ADMIT THE
JOYOUS PASSION
OF REVOLT

Also by Elena Gomez

ADMIT THE JOYOUS PASSION OF REVOLT

Elena Gomez

PUNCHER & WATTMANN

First published in 2020
Published by Puncher and Wattmann
PO Box 279
Waratah NSW 2298

http://www.puncherandwattmann.com
puncherandwattmann@bigpond.com

NATIONAL
LIBRARY
OF AUSTRALIA

A catalogue entry for this book is available from the National Library of Australia.

ISBN   9781925780741

Cover design by Miranda Douglas
Typesetting by Morgan Arnett
Printed by Lightning Source International

I.

Faces flushed from mid morn
jogs behind shipyard
When it's over were you less
inclined to work

Sometimes you think perhaps you haven't
read enough lux theory you need
pure direction
Otherwise you forget   how to

read or chew or where the book goes
or you drop it & there's digression
by our friends down the pipe

ready 2 grow
/
                    ready 2 enable

like how you enable
me to be

demanding of pleasure

we thought a new and brighter future
was just a combo for workers of the world
when worker–mother differentiated
when I read enough novels

'to know how much time and energy it takes to fall in love
and i
     just don't have the time'

spread your torchlight out on all sides   lick a battery
     & the code of practice
like when we woke
Kristen Stewart &   she asked for you
     immediately so
we swaddled her in cotton

still. we needed more magnesium
a waxy mouth was our only answer
we ate in silence while the aproned chatter
  kept motion
in rotation
 piled loose root veg onto plates

suggestion to roast the last Percheron
for its muscle.
We wiped our brows with its tail
Thanked it for refusing

whenever I make a scene it is: always of people gathered.
of food quibbles. of body organs playing up but the next
stage we are on the move. or have a plan or start to take
care of each other
we turned up   in a proceeding
section   feeding each other
berries

Am I too far inwards? Is this a way to conduct a mob?
I'd prefer at this stage if you would just chew my hair and
my vitamins will nourish you
my glasses dirty just how you like

\

lost all

                    pronouns
 in the burnt-out
condominium

Observing a ribbed cream short sleeve maxi—

You would prefer to behold others but there are crisp
crumbs in her filaments   she likes to clasp onto our
boyfriends while they sleep while they do not notice the air
getting thicker while they do not notice the crumbs
filtering through the ducted system

Her judgment takes into account the labour involved
in anger vs the labour involved in disappointment.
She is to be worn by someone who withstands rotating
modules for productivity

If you have a question or problem
relating to your workplace
gather seashells into the shapes of great faces
amenities, physical environment
spread sand into orifices
eye strain, exhaustion, debilitating overuse injuries
procure a jellyfish pillow

My voice are stuck

// are feelings no wait they're balls of discarded objects
that were superseded by technology no wait!   They're
hoarded bobby pins and lip cream or they are a bunch of
snap back caps

They're ready to be weaponised but mums locked that
chest years ago

chests for cracking open like a sternum or else there is a
tin-bowl speech act

Construct your position: leak it smoothly, read the
undersides <these instructions>. A Failed Metonym. The
Transfiguration of Other. Titanic Rising. When We All Fall
Asleep. Blk Girl Soldier.
Titles borrowed
discarded
and are insufficient.

Rinse your mottled wings in this thin liquid   reassign
mud to a flat oaky board
Thick ripples   in skin kept smooth by protected
classifications
The rock where it ends

Tremolo or some audio sundered
An intermittent security

Enter the terms you wish for

Your daily loop
 On   parallel lines
    ::::
Your imagined transcendence
Sometimes you forge yourself
You're fat with the sound or the beauty of words
on the lines and curves how they look   how they feel
in your mouth
You forget how they also work and
what was the point of this all again.
What does aesthetics even do these days   //

<3

I slid my Tail across the pine Surface
Watched a carbonated Organ emerge from
The robust Orifice
I lapped at the Fluids alongside it

Could have made a calico Rug
Instead chewed the corner of the Manuscript
Fondled the Broom nearby

All this time too re-toast the Spelt Bread
Its afterlife, the Carbon. Who else was witness
To the lit Field
Trying to turn out the
Stomach contents of this slayed
Beast
O ...

II.

dear Alexandra no. I mean, dearest. Or instead to my
comrade or to my speaker no even to the mother the not-
mother are you tired yet, is there a way for us to
communicate that won't rely on false memories or feigned
scholarship or mere connection or my own mother
memory asking: where is Inessa?

dear Alexandra o wait my pen has run out of ink

dear Alexandra where did your unpublished stories go

dear Alexandra please where are the new women were the
old women somewhere is the un-born woman anywhere or
does work also abolish the rest

dear Alexandra show me Eros, please

dear Alexandra how many lovers does it take to bring
down an empire

dear Alexandra you are not Lorca (it's okay)

dear Alexandra i cannot pay my rent

dear Alexandra you are not Lenin (thank u)

dear Alexandra will the blood of our children drain
efficiently

dear Alexandra where did all the mystic energy disappear
to

dear Alexandra   ...   pls

dear Alexandra can we interpret dreams with only water
and a small shallow dish

Gently sanding a face with a silk scarf
softly rolling a face into sugared bread buns
                              crystals dissolve

we won't retain you further: this agreement
is getting less desirable by the second.
What is the face of it?
Shall we visit the dining hall?
Is pea protein served in a mass
Pot?

Did you dream about Coach Taylor again the one where he
sits on the side of your bed and runs a finger across your
temple and tells you the university system is a neoliberal
scam so it's okay if you do not want to pursue a career in
higher education

or shall we learn to read a poem without reflux
or re-stitch your hat so it sits over your ears
or——was this the dream where Coach Taylor demands
you carry him downstairs
away from the fire
and the crackling timber
towards the bruised meadow

I covered my face with your hands and with a canvas tote
& also with the leftover newspaper from our children's
play session & I covered my face with woollen clawed
carpet samples and also I did it with plastic leftover and I
covered my face with your refusal to raise wages I covered

my face with a black patterned shawl I covered my face
with the bloodstained bed sheet I covered my

face

with a mulberry lipstick I covered my face with your
softest towel I covered my face with my hands and with a
cowskin purse with a bunch of coins I found in the street
outside your house i

covered my face with I and i covered and I with a wool I
covered your refusal to raise wages I my face I face with
my my face with I covered I covered I covered

my face with Bakunin's abolition of the family my face I
covered with these discarded notes from the meeting of
the first international I covered my face with Zetkin's
sanitary napkin I covered my

face with capsicum seeds I covered my face with red and
gold twine I covered my face it was a feeling of safety I
covered my face you were in the other room I covered my
face I could no longer see and was less distressed I covered
my face with a foolproof plan against timecodes I covered
my face with a large grandfather clock I covered my face
with

the largest spider to crawl out from my bed I covered my
face with toaster dust I covered my face and nobody cared
I covered my face and stormed the winter palace I covered
my face & we all went home and slept in a large bed & I
covered my face & we were pretty safe from feeling at least
for a short while.

III.

My skin is the leotard you left me
When you departed
For the seaside.

Marriage was not capable. My romance
subverted a plot laid heavy with
pristine intention. When a reaction
levels you

I might carefully gaze at your surroundings
Pluck the best of it—masticate.
The choices ahead. Mine is a plump
Desire ready to morph as required.

What would we topple next <after>
: The imperial colossus

Post lunch we must concretise
Or, like, formulate. or vanish

Or something where our actions are worthy of
This oaf writing about us.

Slide up to the pool edge;
Eat a frozen banana shake
while your lover naps

wake
and see how boring this all is

My son is ready
    for manhood   without me. Practice.

Flight.

My son's lives.

Here my birth a ballet dancer

Here my birth a governess: ready to re-educate

the contents of
'too much family happiness'

Agitating.

Here we go

      watching

            a large group

        descend.

To my comrade:
No. To my wife. Or are you my sister. To my moon. Twin.
Or friend.

To you, my love. I'm writing because
I'm sorry. My phone smashed
When we parted ways so violently. I threw it
And it bounced off your bicep and hurtled
Towards the marble statue you ran
To hide behind.

And then my headphones were smashed against an angelic
Face made of stone. You my comrade have a great deal to
learn.

See, the hyena I've been feeding at night was fat
For us soon & it turned out
I learned one night

The hyena had advanced hand-eye coordination. I laughed
At her & she got me with a slingshot that just about
punctured my left nipple.

Could you imagine—my love, my moon—what better
Life had I properly severed your spinal cord
Somehow. What a time commune we could bend into:
A commune to absorb & multiply

Here it is. The flight path announced in the food court
before we board. Can you hear it over the————

We're going to coast on a westerly and revive our style
midair with gin. Ready the combatants with that speech
you do so well.

I'm in that poem where you say we are No Lambs. Not
bees, fighter jets. But tendrils
Thick & twisty & tough & unstoppable. Underground.

I'll forget to pay attention. The vines in my own backyard.
Can someone recall what we named them?

I'm always distracted.

I've got Chelsea Blue jeans.

But I remember. The vine that was ready to escape my
backyard was called Electrolyte. I remembered because I
would wrap it around me when I woke hungover many
mornings.

I want to reclaim the eye
But first these vines in my backyard need tending
They are turning on me they have
Had their loyalty tested by my children.

I want to reclaim.

I was stuck in a whorl

We are on this plane with June and Ariana & your children.
& your rallying speech
Is begun

We're approaching a horizon

But please stop the war imagery that is only
Causing a billowing: a strange rejig of anxiety

To fall right over. My greatest fear. After not working.

Could we visit the ballet instead. You are not
        on trial for your commitment to waging labour war
with a sewing machine.

Your buttons in fact can drop
        into this chute & my mother is
Waiting behind us to assist the revolution in
        this way.

                        needlepoint.

&c.

BREAD & LAND

she is just not yet dead or read to quit

when I cast a spell once using modernity
& yeast
   extract I nearly died.

I was flanked by my moon twin
& revolutionary mother, the woman
who taught us how to disperse
childcare & disregard the spiritualism
of caring. Our moral characters
grew in a sunny classroom with
a large board of cheese & pet rodent
named Zola

It isn't always this windy. Right?
My fingers are bruised & my lips
are chapped. I've carefully layered
shirts & T-shirts & jackets & cardigans
but you brushed past &
I shivered vivid.

Now it is dusk & we can
Land & camp & there are some
Who are better at succour but—

Not me. I can braid a tight one
& offer distraction. Or
even boil an egg

Sometimes we prefer to search
For berries than reorganise the commune.

A keyboard shortcut; you could've said something.
I watched for a bit before we packed up the office.
Whatever else was going on
You were still supreme at note-taking
When pamphlet distribution was at an all-time low
When my rag curls refused to keep up with fashion
I had to work this way so you would think I still loved
you
But I could not love you.

Can you pretend for a moment we are cephalopods
Our tentacles hold the mode of response called for
In this current climate

In this current climate where speech is an act & spring
Has a 'girls in war' kind of vibe now.
I came late to the lab but examined the cell structure
Walls appeared bereft. We'd asked to scrub them

But there was not enough sugar soap in the storeroom.
Remember: the deep dive.
The close crouch you do before you leap onto him.
Your cupped, tight palms.

A girl falls asleep.
Supplement to a family
    income.
Your creation rests.

I sleep uneasy when I'm reading you. I'm unfazed by most
things & I read at an advanced level.
If this is a short history of the working class
in Finland I may travel lightly. Re-pin my bonnet.

Chronic malfunctioning of logic and reasoning. The youth regained

by size. A book. Your face as it rests. A resistance built around the

fibrous qualities of various clothing materials. Or machinery.

A flustered house guest. Salivating unhelpfully. My children chopping

vegetables to prepare our winter feast.

IV.

SO HERE SITS EROS ON WINGS COLLECT YOUR
ENTRY FEE AT THE DOOR WE WAIT FOR
THE NOISE OUT IN THE STREETS TO DIE AWAY
BUT IN THE MEANTIME EROS IS READY FOR A
MEAL

YOUNG POLITE MAN BRINGS EROS A PLATE
OF SEEDLESS GRAPES AND A VEINY BLUE
WHILE IN THE WINGS BEHIND THE STAGE MY
SISTERS FRANTICALLY PATCH THE THROW

13 March 1881
Consider this: an assassination is like a poem
Or if not a poem it is like a speech
Or if not a speech it is like a day off
Or if not a day off it is like a waxed moon
Or if not a waxed moon it is the space between a heartbeat

An assassination is unlike a neat and prepared meal
Nor is it like a dance
Nor is it like a kiss or like winged Eros

An assassination is a comma
A chance to return a gaze
Or sliced limb or two or burst an artery

It is a garden in full bloom or at least
The corner of the garden planted with perennials

We are foisting and a touch
of the plastic sheet written

into the night. Swift heart
readied for a sparse feed

Or wondrous nervous limbs
Are fighting and flying

Is a lush question at the
base of a fountain

at which my creature
rests uneasily
  always

or else planting a golden paw
at the apple trees on the foot

of the hill. Who would we channel
like how I channel the pink

cephalopod
whose approach to

a problem succours
me into dozing

Clusters of remarkable dirt

Circling marble. A doorway.
Entrance – a half
moon like a scented step

You can enter this
Bedroom. I said.
To the man.

I climbed away
A mountain goat
found me weeping
and I refused its offer

Tornado. Swift—a drenched cleanout. Fire. tornado.
things. Are bad. tornado. I smile
Even when I'm not supposed to.

Soft and crumpled satin.
My brain is broken
my employers know it.

I wish to please you as much
as a William Morris print
pleases me.
As much as a twin horn
like H D gave us or else
the second volume of *Capital*

If wind roars beneath an awning
&   like a groan or a wail like
an insistent plea.
persuasive—encapsulating. I could
scream back but I desire
the peace of a power outage.

Your domestic assistance is smooth
Like avocado square tiles
In a Slovenian swimming pool.

Your hallowed space strong
M reaching for a
peeled fruit

Hilda's palimpsest could
afford us an answer

had we dug. had I
heard. Or else the

mantra remains

be heavy

drop hips &
bard teeth. I'm in love.

If we sit here and light
a candle and I open
a box of snacks and
we concoct our new
system that is not a
prayer or a theology

it is not a print
for love stories or
baby manuals or a
booklet about how
to clip the wings of
eros. not a crew
set off to skin some
sea animals to feed
a fledgling campsite.

not a creed or fawn
child or story
of Arthurian proportions

The brown rice
you singled out

there's a statue
frowned at
sits in the market
follows us home
reminding everyone that you
still reward complicit
violence

My fingers are so plump
Can I place in your mouth
            Silos, filled &
Fostered through childhood—my face is all lot
Now what have you done
       to me.

We are not locked but mobile
         Fly Traps reaching a
limit of atmospheric heights

did you forget the contract
the intern he buried beneath
the ferns

after a boss leaked his failures
through the air vents

After a boss leaked the surplus
labour all over your standing desk

we divided the chips from my
snack pockets. I was too girly

and it showed.

My muslin dress helped but I wanted it.

You were too hesitant and the
possum who lived inside the roof could
tell we are too afraid to climb

and then there is barbarism
& savagery & barbarism or
the barbarity of marriage pursuant
to the centuries

she hurts

mine is a special sort of revolt

a revolt where there's no future
& we need the scientists not the
scientists but THESCIENTISTS

a dolewave or slacker band from
north west Melbourne maybe sunbury
or a bit closer not so west
   maybe preston

the band that sings glum about going
to work every day but not about writing
letters to our dead poetmothers

or even reconstruct the poetmother
& see how I reproduce the structures
& cannot change it

And later we hid under the meeting
Room floor & exchanged notes &
Snacks contractually implicated in
Plotting session nicknamed sao paolo

I read a poem by _____ out loud to you
You said it reminded you of my poems
I was flattered & embarrassed bc this was a
V Good Poet

We joked to our reading group that we could
write our way to a revolution
Except it wasn't a we it was a me
Except it wasn't our reading group it was empty
Except it wasn't a joke it was a bad novel series pitch
Except it wasn't a revolution

Except   we didn't write

In my thirtieth year except
it is the fortieth year of my mother
becoming a mother

There is a question surrounding us i.e. how many poems
will recuperate the surplus value produced by a worker
who must read in order to produce the company's
commodity

Our heroine: choose between prison & military to pass into
adulthood

The preoccupation with snacks over meals iow snacks as
portable & diverse/snacks as the precariat food source or
snacks as post-revolution family structure to replace the
sturdy & historically stable MEAL. Snacks & their position
in a hierarchy of nourishment are you standing all day or
moving round are you a still sitter.

                                                        Work for us

Hemlock

                Lunate bone
Home insulator kit, a window
The dark

   An hour stole back

[nonwork/antiwork/postwork futures]

slick lint cover : the cat mask
or, a superior tilt (my hips redirected)
 or a list poem
  or a discard pile
   or else the desk
    or a shoulder stretch

my body a site of

    composition

                here, or,

in sheet music manuscripts
this is clumsy sorry
I need to verify this

at 0625

        or 0618

A series of poems with a significant date
title system overrides yr flanked entrance
Gig Ryan: January
The end of one and here it
Gains work / or us against work
I produce a sonnet & it sits apart
Here a decline of an empire is
The title of every history book written
I cannot prophesise a Secondsummer
Regeneration where the flowering reoccurs
Or the pollinator fluctuations are monitored
Until we depart the new colony inspection
For it is not a dialogue or here it is not at least
But we might also argue in four-part choral score

My death / my death

When I sat here & my background music came forward. I
paused the pink noise playlist, I put on Scott Walker.

I paused my poem. I picked up the paper. I remembered
RED MARS and about Arkady's death, his combusting
arm. Maya's world crumbling.

The seminar where a Marxist gave a paper about Kim
Stanley Robinson's Mars trilogy & how it took me another
three to four years before I found the books myself.

The 8-point font of a b format.
The noticeable double space here, there, occasional.

Scott Walker's *Tilt* on repeat now. Arkady's death.
Combusting arm.

The black hole photograph. The woman whose
calculations helped give this to us.

When my revolution idea based itself on test tubes, &c.
decolonisation. The flattened genders.

I am meant to be thinking about revolution RIGHT NOW
but all I can think of is outer space. And Arkady's
combusting arm.

How else a subjectivity is leaked out: the things we are
reading that we returned to. My circular thoughts. The
determination: Maddy and Dion telling us they just want to
be able to go about in public without the world assigning
them as parents and denying them non-parent spaces. This
is worse for the mothers. But sometimes fathers too.

How everyone was a child once and yet forgets it &
how children aren't welcome in the public
world. That they are designated.

How the brief hours I spent caring for my nephews made
me love them more, and at the same strengthened my
resolve to not become a mother in my lifetime.

Have I read too much Kollontai now.

What if I'm old

I'm allowed to put myself here. In the place of time, we
have sunken convex couch cushions.

I set myself the time. I borrow the clock-based
productivity methods from my boyfriend.

I borrow the apps. I borrow an hour & a dozing afternoon.

Insoluble (or body heat) is the description on the label
Forget the steam dryer. This one is a whole closet!

I construct a history of clothes in the form of a novel
From the p.o.v. of a removable collar (before washing
machines

Altered the temporal composition of a working day)
I reread *Bartelby* and forge, a revolutionary, Google shared
doc

For office workers. & office cleaners. The right mix of
course.

Nobody believes me when I tell them: my cat enjoys to
watch me

Fail at this. She has few opinions outside her feeding times
but

we often turn to each other & engage psychically. She does
not

understand me & I don't understand her & we are happily
co

habiters & nobody tries to anthropomorphise her. But
sometimes

I come home to rewatch Jurassic Park for the fifty-
somethingth time

& she watches with me. We don't like the cages.

It's structured
though a hunting instinct
My discarded crust. The dome.

Who else is present for starters
The organisers. My day off.

The unwashed coffee pot.
How else would the meeting begin

What is the game play in this situation

A scenario. List-making.

Collaborative or adversarial?

A celestial body wreaks havoc
This personal gravity, here take my staff,
Credentials waved around: your hat rim.
Meanwhile our veins are luminous like
Deep ocean dwellers. Our biology intact.
For now. & my wood-free stock paper
not so limb-hugging as we first thought—

My chaotic heart is contractual obligation
   It is this or else met with punitive
Measures. My chaotic heart resides in the kitchen
   It is forever kept on low constant heat

Sprung here fresh a glitter rush
Cartilage removed for lack of use value

The urchins gather at my feet & sink into
Sand alongside the sunset & my notifications
    On silence

Gatherings for a flat pack removal surface
A rental truck & my mother
A 2BR apartment lease

blonde woman: clothes and house décor is white and beige.
jewelry, crystal light fittings. Excess is very white money.
Rih kidnaps the woman. The woman is strung, naked, in
the warehouse, and taunted by the assistant.

Convertible on fire.

Rih on a boat now. Pool party: inflatables.

Fires a flare gun (rih)
Wears fur muff.
Girl back to motel room. She is blindfolded and made up
bongs camera angle either lots of short cuts or angled
movement. They are making her up, curlers in hair, getting
her drunk and high.

The cop returns. They hide the woman every time.

Try to think a little every day. It won't hurt. Until it does.
Think more carefully: what kind of poetry are you making?
Why is this so hard to contemplate?

It's a Courtney Love babydoll dress in peach.

Or large black ungainly frock gathered in one hand.

A piano in the corner. A stage facing the crowd.

Could you shout more or are we sufficient

It's a lavender pillow mist—Or else militant sincerity.

When we debated Contracts & The Future. If there was a

way around bosses. And household statistics.

It all came back to the same thing.

Here my constraints
Reckon with   time

Our places flipped against
A wall a curve a soft
                    Ground

Diana Hamilton asking solid questions about animals.

He spent the night sharpening my left hook as I slept.

We are spilling out love. It is taxable.

Care & the collective heart. My poetry is insignificant.

Remember you have your own advice: there are animals
and they need us.

Acknowledgements

This book was written on the unceded lands of the Gadigal people of the Eora nation and the Wurundjeri and Boonwurrung people of the Kulin nation. It originated as a practice-based research project for the Master of Fine Arts in Poetry, which was completed at UNSW Art & Design under supervisors Dr Astrid Lorange and Dr Verónica Tello. The book's title comes from Ewa Ziarek's *Feminist Aesthetics and the Politics of Modernism* (2012). I am immensely grateful to Astrid and Veronica for their advice and support over the years.

Thank you to my poetry communities, especially those who were part of the making of this book through reading, conversing and communing about poetry, aesthetics, communism and Marxist feminism: Andrew Brooks, Amy De'Ath, Romi Graham, Leah Muddle, Ella O'Keefe, Melody Paloma, Juliana Spahr, Lindsay Turner, Sian Vate, Tim Wright and others.

I thank my parents for everything, and I offer this book in memory of Malcolm Gomez (19.10.47–24.8.19).

I thank Ann Vickery for her encouragement and support, and for her poetry, and I thank Puncher & Wattmann for bringing this book into the world.

Finally, thank you to my partner, Rory Dufficy, who was immeasurably patient and generous with his support while I wrote. I thank him for sharing the gift of his sharp ear for poetry. The revolution is still to come but, until then, I am grateful to have such an intelligent, clear-headed and loving person with whom to navigate the pitfalls of capitalism.